Love

This edition first published in 2020
Carrington Allen
www.carringtonallenart.com

ISBN 978-1-71665-560-9

Published by Made With Words
Created by Carrington Allen
www.carringtonallenart.com

Printed in the United States of America

Love

Carrington Allen

Dedicated to all of those brave enough to love unconditionally, to accept themselves with gratitude and grace, and to extend the same to others.

Gratitude to Source for inspiration and collaboration. And appreciation to my mother, Emily, Sophie and Matthew for an abundance of encouragement. A special thank you to Emily for her extraordinary editing.

Thoughts to share

This book is about love, healing, and discovering more about yourself and what life should be for all of us.

We each hold great wisdom in our hearts, and it is my desire to inspire others to realize and pursue their potential.

I hope these words bring you to a place of reflection. May you be filled with peace and hope for the future. And may you be blessed to feel the love that exists in your life.

Love

This book of love is presented to you
To assist you to find what is true

Words upon a page to make the truth so clear
To guide you within, to draw you near

To see what life is meant to be
When once you realize you are truly free

Free from debt, from man-made rules
Free to go where your heart pulls

Love is simply all, not none
It's everywhere and never done.

Love is the beginning
and the end.

All life is created from divine love
and will one day return
to divine love.

Love inhabits every human body on a cellular level.

Derived from many parts forming a link of sorts, it transforms a child from the moment of birth.

Not one but two, appearing as duplicates, these chromosomes bring about a foundation of life.

The duality of the masculine and the feminine that give life to each child are represented in this chromosome.

Wholeness of this chromosome is necessary for this foundation to support a lifetime of health and well-being.

Without adjustment or mending, this foundation can become weak, resulting in deficiencies.

The inherited copies of this chromosome
found in duplicate can be altered
simply by requesting
the innate self.

This message about love is generated at a time when humanity appears lost, caught between turmoil and angst.

A time when communities do not care for one another because they do not know one another.

Love has been lost because connection has been lost or disrupted.

The channels of communication that once brought people together face to face have been replaced with technology. And in case you have yet to notice, you cannot feel the true energy of love and connection through a cell phone or a computer screen.

Love is a personal thing. In fact, it begins with your own self image.

How can you expect anyone to cherish,
respect and be inspired by you
if you can't cherish, respect, or inspire
yourself?

To heal the world,
you must first heal
yourself.

To heal yourself,
you must first love yourself.

To love yourself,
you must see
and understand
your soul self.

Love of self is at the center
or core of healing.

You hold the key to healing.

But first there is work to do before you reach the door.

You must first lighten your load...

There are certain things you cannot carry with you any longer.

Some are outdated beliefs, behaviors, emotions, and thought patterns.

Humanity has been lectured to, punished, and held in captivity by egoistic leadership for thousands of years.

It is time to release all of these energies to allow you to move forward to level up, to raise your vibration, to move closer to becoming the light soul beings you are destined for.

Time now is of the essence to heal yourselves and your children, to release the suffering, the Karma, and the contracts.

These energies were collected as a result of choices made with free will. The same free will you still have today.

You have the free will to continue to choose suffering and hardships or choose light and love.

No one can make the choice for you, nor should you ever allow anyone to choose for you.

Free will

This is your greatest freedom.

Every person
on earth
is granted
free will
at birth.

Which brings the question -
quite a moment of reflection...

Up to this moment in your life,

"How have you
used your free will?"

Have you chosen
a life of love and light
guided by truth
and wisdom?

Or have you
occasionally
stumbled in fear
and darkness
guided by desire
and greed?

In this moment,
what does your heart guide
you to choose?

Fear?
or
Love?

Darkness?
or
Light?

Those that choose
suffering
will not heal.

Those that choose
fear
will not heal.

Source never forces
a certain choice,
but knows
choosing anything
other than light and love
will eventually
bring you back
to another chance
to choose
light and love again.

Your choice to follow the path
of fear and darkness
will always bring you
to moments or opportunities
to rise to a higher path.

The choice is always yours,
your birthright - free will.

Choosing love
is your
first step
to healing
your mind,
body,
and soul.

By choosing love,
you walk a path of truth,
compassion, and integrity.

A life of service to others,
to contributing to the highest good
for all humanity and planet earth.

A big decision,
but one that quickly
simplifies your life.

With nothing to hide
and everything to gain,
you will live a life
of abundance,
loyalty, and honesty,
leading you to live
your soul's authentic
divine purpose.

After choosing love,
you must connect to love.

To connect you must know...

What is love?
Love is Source.

Where is love?
Love is
within everything
and within nothing.

Why is love?
Love is to create life.

Who is love?
Love is you.

How do we connect to love?

You connect to love
by listening to your intuition,
by talking to your higher self.

Some call this prayer.

Some call this meditation.

Some call this talking to yourself.

How do you receive messages?

You practice.

Start in a quiet place,
and clear your thoughts.

Focus on breathing and slowly calm,
positive thoughts will seep in.

Just listen,
for Source has much
to share with you.

Practice day after day, making this connection, strengthening your ability to clearly receive your intuitive guidance.

With practice you will be able to easily connect throughout your day to seek Source's input or knowledge or guidance.

Your connection to this infinite love will begin to heal your body and your life.

Follow Source's guidance to heal and align your body and its energies.

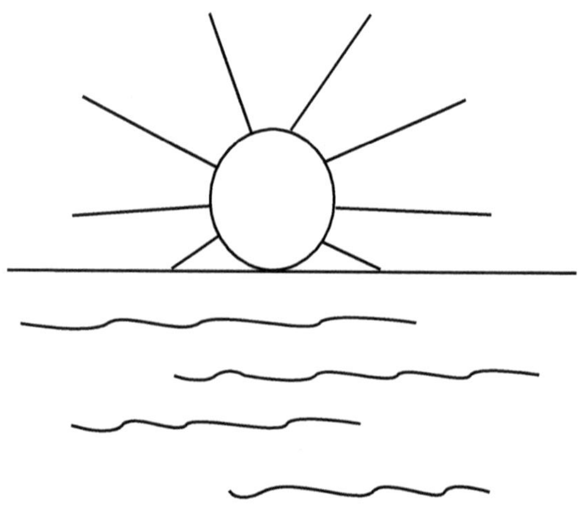

Guidance
is needed
to begin to heal.

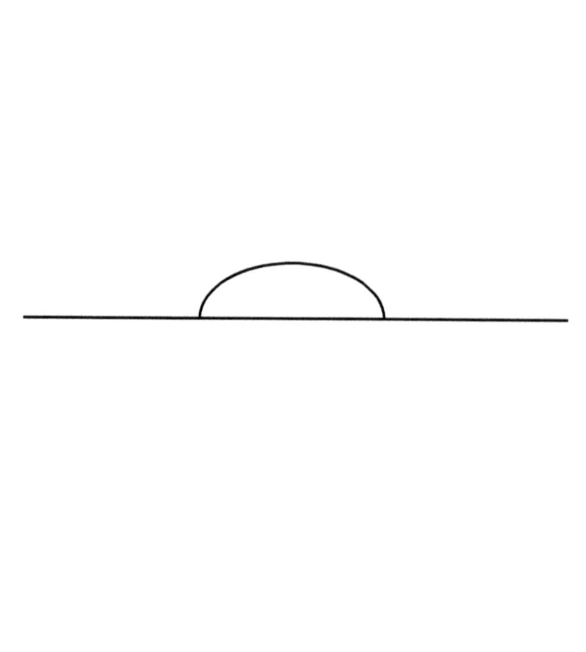

Without guidance,
you may not know where to start
or what truly needs healing -
not only within your body
but within your life
and your relationships.

Starting with
a strong
positive sense
of self is best,
but
most of humanity
will begin
from
a much lower,
denser energy
or place.

These dense energies control the vibrational level of each cell within your body.

And this vibration has the ability to manifest health or disease depending on how quickly it vibrates.

The faster the movement, the more easily it repels negativity.

Therefore, raising or increasing vibration is the ultimate goal.

Many have been led to
believe that just thinking
positive thoughts
will solve this dilemma
of how to raise your vibration.

It is true, this helps.

It is also true
that other contributing factors
are not only more important
but also longer lasting
with a greater impact.

As mentioned, to heal you must choose love and light. This requires truly walking this path daily, moment to moment using your free will to enhance every corner of your life.

By living this authentic life, you will supply your mind, body, and soul with the resources needed to not only sustain itself but also to evolve and grow into the best version of yourself.

When faced with challenges,
your intuition will easily guide
you in the best direction.

This guidance
will enable you
to remain balanced,
and balance
is the key
to successfully healing
and bringing
your entire system
into alignment.

Once you have balanced
your internal self,
it will be time
to mend
your external
environment.

This brings many challenges
that will often leave you
focusing only on how you choose
to react and connect
with these external
negative influences.

Ranging from horrific movie content to jarring song lyrics, your media has contributed vast amounts of damaging energy to your cells.

Removing, or at least restricting, your exposure is necessary to avoid further damage and illness.

Removing yourself from negative environments will immediately raise your vibration. The power of protecting your energy's vibrational frequency cannot be stressed enough.

You must understand, low vibration attracts negative energies and outcomes. As important as choosing love and light, raising and protecting your energy level is your key to survival.

Along your healing journey you will find many helpful tools. I offer you a few here to discover:

plant-based foods
grounding
prayer/meditation
walking
sunrise/sunset energy
cooking with love
compassion

Utilize these tools to improve your life and the lives of those around you.

Everything
you need to heal,
to live,
to evolve
is within your reach.

It is up to you,
your choice,
your
free will.

Healing is a life-long journey
of self discovery.

A ladder, of sorts,
to climb one step at a time,
careful to keep your balance
focusing on your current
place and step.

As you ascend this ladder,
you will attain
sacred knowledge.

You will learn to
practice acting with compassion.

You will learn to see
the benevolence in others
and understand how their challenges
create their digressions.

You will strive to lead
by example
without
egoistic judgment.

These strengths
will flow quietly
unnoticed
into your life
until one day
you awake
with
a sense of peace,
tranquility,
and
sincere
love for life.

Your
perseverance,
courage,
and patience
will bring you
to a place of flow.

A sense of calm.

Your heartbeat
will become one
with the waves
of the ocean,
and your request
to be connected
to the Divine
will be
granted.

Your healing journey
will continue as you
live your days
in service to others.

You have acquired
the wisdom
that as long as your heart
is beating,
you can still inspire
and give hope to others.

It is never too late
to choose Source.

When you choose Source,
you choose love.

You are the only one that can
make the choice.

And in the end it is the only
choice left.

Love is
the Alpha
and the Omega.

Love is
all
you will find
in the end.

Notes from your soul's journey…

www.ingramcontent.com/pod-product-compliance
Ingram Content Group UK Ltd.
Pitfield, Milton Keynes, MK11 3LW, UK
UKHW020219250726
13967UKWH00001B/81

9 781716 655609